T0352108

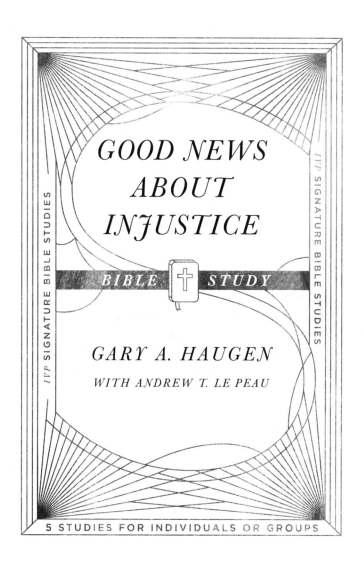

GOOD NEWS ABOUT INJUSTICE

BIBLE ✝ *STUDY*

GARY A. HAUGEN

WITH ANDREW T. LE PEAU

IVP SIGNATURE BIBLE STUDIES

IVP SIGNATURE BIBLE STUDIES

5 STUDIES FOR INDIVIDUALS OR GROUPS

An imprint of InterVarsity Press
Downers Grove, Illinois

InterVarsity Press
P.O. Box 1400, Downers Grove, IL 60515-1426
ivpress.com
email@ivpress.com

InterVarsity Press® is the book-publishing division of InterVarsity Christian Fellowship/USA®, a movement of students and faculty active on campus at hundreds of universities, colleges, and schools of nursing in the United States of America, and a member movement of the International Fellowship of Evangelical Students. For information about local and regional activities, visit intervarsity.org.

All Scripture quotations, unless otherwise indicated, are taken from The Holy Bible, New International Version®, NIV®. Copyright © 1973, 1978, 1984, 2011 by Biblica, Inc.™ Used by permission of Zondervan. All rights reserved worldwide. www.zondervan.com. The "NIV" and "New International Version" are trademarks registered in the United States Patent and Trademark Office by Biblica, Inc.™

While any stories in this book are true, some names and identifying information may have been changed to protect the privacy of individuals.

This study guide is based on and adapts material from Good News About Injustice, *Tenth Anniversary Edition by Gary A Haugen, ©2009 by International Justice Mission.*

Cover design and image composite: David Fassett
Interior design: Daniel van Loon
Image: Blurred candle © Tim Umphreys@timumphreys

ISBN 978-0-8308-4845-4 (print)
ISBN 978-0-8308-4846-1 (digital)

Printed in the United States of America ♾

InterVarsity Press is committed to ecological stewardship and to the conservation of natural resources in all our operations. This book was printed using sustainably sourced paper.

P 21 20 19 18 17 16 15 14 13 12 11 10 9 8 7 6 5 4 3 2 1

Y 39 38 37 36 35 34 33 32 31 30 29 28 27 26 25 24 23 22 21

CONTENTS

GETTING
THE MOST OUT OF

GOOD NEWS ABOUT INJUSTICE
BIBLE STUDY

KNOWING CHRIST is where faith begins. From there we are shaped through the essentials of discipleship: Bible study, prayer, Christian community, worship, and much more. We learn to grow in Christlike character, pursue justice, and share our faith with others. We persevere through doubts and gain wisdom for daily life. These are the topics woven into the IVP Signature Bible Studies. Working through this series will help you practice the essentials by exploring biblical truths found in classic books.

HOW IT'S PUT TOGETHER

Each session includes an opening quotation and suggested reading from the book *Good News About Injustice*, a session goal to help guide your study, reflection questions to stir your thoughts on the topic, the text of the Bible passage, questions for exploring the passage, response questions to help you apply what you've learned, and a closing suggestion for prayer.

The workbook format is ideal for personal study and also allows group members to prepare in advance for discussions and record discussion notes. The responses you write here can form a permanent record of your thoughts and spiritual progress.

Throughout the guide are study-note sidebars that may be useful for group leaders or individuals. These notes do not give the answers, but they do provide additional background information on certain questions and can challenge participants to think deeper or differently about the content.

WHAT KIND OF GUIDE IS THIS?

The studies are not designed to merely tell you what one person thinks. Instead, through inductive study, they will help you discover for yourself what Scripture is saying. Each study deals with a particular passage—rather than jumping around the Bible—so that you can really delve into the biblical author's meaning in that context.

The studies ask three different kinds of questions about the Bible passage:

* *Observation* questions help you to understand the content of the passage by asking about the basic facts: who, what, when, where, and how.

* *Interpretation* questions delve into the meaning of the passage.

* *Application* questions help you discover implications for growing in Christ in your own life.

These three keys unlock the treasures of the biblical writings and help you live them out.

This is a thought-provoking guide. Each question assumes a variety of answers. Many questions do not have "right" answers, particularly questions that aim at meaning or application. Instead, the questions should inspire readers to explore the passage more thoroughly.

This study guide is flexible. You can use it for individual study, but it is also great for a variety of groups—student, professional, neighborhood, or church groups. Each study takes about forty-five minutes in a group setting or thirty minutes in personal study.

SUGGESTIONS FOR INDIVIDUAL STUDY

1. This guide is based on a classic book that will enrich your spiritual life. If you have not read *Good News About Injustice*, you may want to read the portion recommended in the "Read" section before you begin your study. The ideas in the book will enhance your study, but the Bible text will be the focus of each session.

2. Begin each session with prayer, asking God to speak to you from his Word about this particular topic.

3. As you read the Scripture passage, reproduced for you from the New International Version, you may wish to mark phrases that seem important. Note in the margin any questions that come to your mind.

4. Close with the suggested prayer found at the end of each session. Speak to God about insights you have gained. Tell him of any desires you have for specific growth. Ask him to help you attempt to live out the principles described in that passage. You may wish to write your own prayer in this guide or a journal.

SUGGESTIONS FOR GROUP MEMBERS

Joining a Bible study group can be a great avenue to spiritual growth. Here are a few guidelines that will help you as you participate in the studies in this guide.

1. Reading the recommended portion of *Good News About Injustice*, before or after each session, will enhance your study and understanding of the themes in this guide.

2. These studies use methods of inductive Bible study, which focuses on a particular passage of Scripture and works on it in depth. So try to dive into the given text instead of referring to other Scripture passages.

3. Questions are designed to help a group discuss together a passage of Scripture in order to understand its content, meaning, and implications. Most people are either natural talkers or natural listeners, yet this type of study works best if all members participate more or less evenly. Try to curb any natural tendency toward either excessive talking or excessive quiet. You and the rest of the group will benefit!

4. Most questions in this guide allow for a variety of answers. If you disagree with someone else's comment, gently say so. Then explain your own point of view from the passage before you.

5. Be willing to lead a discussion, if asked. Much of the preparation for leading has already been accomplished in the writing of this guide.

6. Respect the privacy of people in your group. Many people share things within the context of a Bible study group that they do not want to be public knowledge. Assume that personal information spoken within the group setting is private, unless you are specifically told otherwise.

7. We recommend that all groups agree on a few basic guidelines. You may wish to adapt this list to your situation:

   a. Anything said in this group is considered confidential and will not be discussed outside the group unless specific permission is given to do so.

   b. We will provide time for each person present to talk if he or she feels comfortable doing so.

    c. We will talk about ourselves and our own situations, avoiding conversation about other people.

    d. We will listen attentively to each other.

    e. We will pray for each other.

8. Enjoy your study. Prepare to grow!

SUGGESTIONS FOR GROUP LEADERS

There are specific suggestions to help you in the "Leading a Small Group" section. It describes how to lead a group discussion, gives helpful tips on group dynamics, and suggests ways to deal with problems that may arise during the discussion. With such helps, someone with little or no experience can lead an effective group study. Read this section carefully, even if you are leading only one group meeting.

INTRODUCTION

DISCOVERING THE GOD OF JUSTICE

I DON'T HAVE THE PRIVILEGE OF KNOWING where each of you may be in your own journey of faith. I feel like I've been trying to follow Jesus for a long time—since I was a little boy. Growing up, I could not have been further from all the ugly abuse in the world. I was born in Sacramento, California, the spoiled youngest of six children with a dad who was a doctor and a mom who made sure we all went to church about thirteen times a week.

Looking back, I am so grateful for that childhood and all it formed in me, but the truth is that realities of terror, oppression, abuse, and injustice were kept far from my door. And, despite hearing at least a thousand sermons growing up, I never once heard a sermon about God's heart for justice, about a holy God who spends his days weeping beside children in brothels, prisoners in pain, or orphans in trauma—a God who hates injustice. I knew little about the needs of the world or how God regards such suffering. I knew even less about what those needs had to do with me or how I could make a difference.

As I went to university in a large urban center, it was the first time I engaged the world of poverty and homelessness. My eyes opened to global issues of violent injustice. In the years since, I have had opportunity to continue to engage these issues, as I have lived in places where there was no escaping the raw realities of a world in rebellion against its Maker—apartheid in South Africa, guerilla war in the Philippines, and genocide in Rwanda. In each of these places I met followers of Jesus Christ who knew God more deeply, knew the Bible more thoroughly, and lived life more courageously than I had ever seen before. It was so clear they actually believed the things God said were true and they staked their lives on it.

If you find yourself in a place where pain in the world feels quite far from you, or too abstract, or perhaps even overwhelmingly familiar, I hope this study helps our hearts grow to become more like the heart of God—a heart that shares something of his interests and passion for the world. I've been on this journey for forty years, accompanied by excellent guides and faithful friends who have sought to understand more deeply both what the Bible says about the God of justice and what it looks like to join God in his work of justice in the world. Because this experience has been miraculously transformational for me, I am passionate about others encountering these truths. I want everyone to have a chance to discover the God of justice who cares for the widow and orphan, the poor and oppressed, the hungry and imprisoned, and the victims of violence.

That is what this Bible study guide is all about. It is a companion to my book *Good News About Injustice,* which tells a story based on Scripture about our fallen world. This guide is an opportunity to see for ourselves who this God is and how he cares for those who have suffered because of injustice.

My prayer for us is that, in this world of so much suffering and hurt and need, we might take hold of this good news about injustice—the good news that God is against it. He is offering to rescue us from trivial things and from all things of fear, and to move us with courage out into this world that is yearning to see the goodness of God in us.

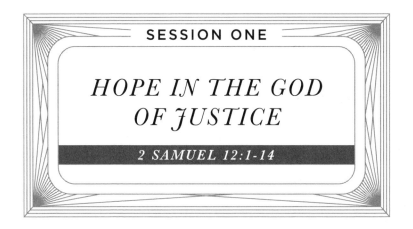

HOPE IN THE GOD OF JUSTICE

2 SAMUEL 12:1-14

THE CENTERPIECE OF OUR HOPE is the revelation from the Almighty that he is a God of justice. As the prophet Isaiah declared, "The LORD is a God of justice. / Blessed are all who wait for him!" (Isaiah 30:18). Justice is fundamental to the holiness of God. "For I, the LORD, love justice," declares our Maker (Isaiah 61:8).

But what does this mean?

To say God is a God of justice means he cares about the right exercise of power and authority. God is the ultimate power and authority in the universe, so justice occurs when power and authority are exercised in conformity with God's standards. In fact, in the Old Testament the Hebrew words for *justice* and *righteousness* are almost interchangeable, both indicating a conformity to God's standards of holiness or moral excellence. Ultimately, the sovereign God of the universe will establish justice over all peoples and spirits because at that time all power and authority in the cosmos will be exercised in accordance with God's standards of moral clarity.

Our God loves justice. This is the great hope that allows Christians to be a mighty force for justice in a tired, despairing world.

SESSION GOAL	READING
To learn to love people who are vulnerable in a way that emulates the God of justice.	*Good News About Injustice* preface and chapters 1 and 4

 **REFLECT**

✳ How would you define or describe justice?

✳ How does it give you hope knowing that God loves justice?

 **STUDY**

READ 2 SAMUEL 12:1-14.

¹The LORD sent Nathan to David. When he came to him, he said, "There were two men in a certain town, one rich and the other poor. ²The rich man had a very large number of sheep and cattle, ³but the poor man had nothing except one little ewe lamb he had bought. He raised it, and it grew up with him and his children. It shared his food, drank from his cup and even slept in his arms. It was like a daughter to him.

⁴"Now a traveler came to the rich man, but the rich man refrained from taking one of his own sheep or cattle to prepare a meal for the traveler who had come to him. Instead, he took the ewe lamb that belonged to the poor man and prepared it for the one who had come to him."

⁵David burned with anger against the man and said to Nathan, "As surely as the LORD lives, the man who did this must die! ⁶He must pay for that lamb four times over, because he did such a thing and had no pity."

⁷Then Nathan said to David, "You are the man! This is what the LORD, the God of Israel, says: 'I anointed you king over Israel, and I delivered you from the hand of Saul. ⁸I gave your master's house to you, and your master's wives into your arms. I gave you all Israel and Judah. And if all this had been too little, I would have given you even more. ⁹Why did you despise the word of the LORD by doing what is evil in his eyes? You struck down Uriah the Hittite with the sword and took his wife to be your own. You killed him with the sword of the Ammonites. ¹⁰Now, therefore, the sword will never depart from your house, because you despised me and took the wife of Uriah the Hittite to be your own.'

¹¹"This is what the LORD says: 'Out of your own household I am going to bring calamity on you. Before your very eyes I will take your wives and give them to one who is close to you, and he will sleep with your wives in broad daylight. ¹²You did it in secret, but I will do this thing in broad daylight before all Israel.'"

¹³Then David said to Nathan, "I have sinned against the LORD."

Nathan replied, "The LORD has taken away your sin. You are not going to die. ¹⁴But because by doing this you have shown utter contempt for the LORD, the son born to you will die."

We learn from the backstory in 2 Samuel 11 that after King David abused his kingly power and authority to possess

Bathsheba, Uriah's wife, she told him she was pregnant. David then tried to cover up the affair by bringing Uriah home from battle for a few days so he would sleep with Bathsheba and therefore assume he (Uriah) was the father. When that failed, David secretly ordered Uriah to be put on the front lines so he would die in battle against the Ammonites.

1. After Bathsheba's child is born, the prophet Nathan confronts David. What does Nathan do to arouse David's rage about injustice?

2. What stories of injustice have incensed you?

3. Why are stories often more effective in motivating us to act than just statistics or reasoned persuasion?

> Injustice occurs when power is misused to take from others what God has given them—their life, dignity, liberty, or the fruits of their love and labor. As it says in Ecclesiastes: "Again I looked and saw all the oppression that was taking place under the sun: I saw the tears of the oppressed—and they have no comforter; power was on the side of their oppressors" (Ecclesiastes 4:1). Injustice is the strong taking from the weak, through means of force and deceit.

4. How does Nathan say his story parallels David's actions?

How did prophets like Nathan think about justice? And who did they think were the primary beneficiaries of justice? Two passages from Jeremiah offer a clue: "If you really change your ways and your actions and deal with each other justly, if you do not oppress the foreigner, the fatherless or the widow and do not shed innocent blood in this place, and if you do not follow other gods to your own harm, then I will let you live in this place, in the land I gave your ancestors for ever and ever" (Jeremiah 7:5-7). "This is what the LORD says: Do what is just and right. Rescue from the hand of the oppressor the one who has been robbed. Do no wrong or violence to the foreigner, the fatherless or the widow, and do not shed innocent blood in this place" (Jeremiah 22:3).

5. The Lord notes how generous he has been with David (2 Samuel 12:7-8). How has God been generous with you?

6. What consequences does God say will come on David as a result of his sin?

> The Word of God tells us God has not
> forgotten injustice done to or the suffering of victims.
> The psalmist asks: "Why does the wicked man revile
> God? Why does he say to himself, 'He won't call me to
> account'? But you, God, see the trouble of the afflicted;
> you consider their grief and take it in hand. The
> victims commit themselves to you; you are the
> helper of the fatherless" (Psalm 10:13-14).

7. How does David respond to the Lord's rebuke through Nathan?

8. What do we learn about God through this story about David and Nathan?

RESPOND

✳ How do you respond to this passage? Explain.

✳ The Bible says our passion for justice and the defense of the weak will reflect how well we know God. "'Did your father . . . do justice and righteousness? Then it was well for him. He pled the cause of the afflicted and the poor, then it was well. Is that not what it means to know Me?' declares the LORD" (Jeremiah 22:15-16 NASB). In what ways have you responded to the plight of the weak, poor, or oppressed in your community, nation, or the world?

 **PRAY**

O God of justice, we praise you that you love what is right and good; you uphold the downtrodden, the poor, the weak. We thank you, knowing this gives us such hope when we see oppression and violence all around us. We know you are at work in the world to help the needy and oppose those who would exploit the vulnerable. Father, may your will be done on earth as it is in heaven. Amen.

NEXT STEPS

Here are some sites that offer a starting point for research on current developments and issues in human rights.

International Justice Mission, ijm.org

A21, a21.org

Amnesty International, amnesty.org/en

Equal Justice Initiative, eji.org

Free Burma Rangers, freeburmarangers.org

Freedom House, freedomhouse.org

Human Rights First, humanrightsfirst.org

Human Rights Watch, hrw.org

The International Criminal Court, icc-cpi.int

International Labour Organization, ilo.org

Polaris Project, polarisproject.org

Preemptive Love, preemptivelove.org

U.N. High Commissioner for Human Rights, ohchr.org

U.S. State Department, and Office to Monitor and Combat Trafficking in Persons, state.gov

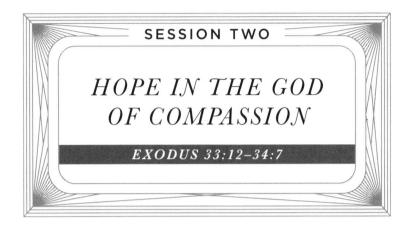

HOPE IN THE GOD OF COMPASSION

EXODUS 33:12–34:7

THE SECOND FUNDAMENTAL TRUTH God wants us to count on in a world of injustice is that God has compassion for those who suffer injustice. Their cries move God. We have hope because we know we serve such a God. "Our God is full of compassion," says the psalmist (Psalm 116:5). He is "the Father of compassion," says the apostle Paul (2 Corinthians 1:3).

The word *compassion* comes from two Latin words: *passio* meaning "to suffer," and *cum* meaning "with." To say God has compassion for the victims of injustice is to say he actually "suffers with" them.

Over and over in the Scriptures, God lets us know he sees and hears the suffering of the oppressed. When the strong abuse their power to take from those who are weaker, the sovereign God of the universe is watching and suffering.

> If you take your neighbor's cloak as a pledge, return it by sunset, because that cloak is the only covering your neighbor has. What else can they sleep in? When they cry out to me, I will hear, for I am compassionate. (Exodus 22:26-27)

> The LORD is a refuge for the oppressed. . . . He does not ignore the cries of the afflicted. (Psalm 9:9, 12)

Look! The wages you failed to pay the workers who mowed your fields are crying out against you. The cries of the harvesters have reached the ears of the Lord Almighty. (James 5:4)

God's compassion for the victims of injustice extends to all people, all around the world, without distinction or favor. While it may seem more natural to have compassion for those closest to us, we won't find in the Bible Jesus asking us to have more compassion for our immediate neighbors or our compatriots than for anyone else. I believe he understands our tendency to do so, but he is probably eager for us to reach out as we are able (or as we seek God's enabling) beyond our carnal limitations, prejudices, cultural mythologies, and convenient stereotypes. Jesus calls us to be witnesses of God's love, truth, salvation, compassion, and justice "in Jerusalem [at home], and in all Judea and Samaria [nearby], and to the ends of the earth" (Acts 1:8).

SESSION GOAL	READING
To better know the compassion of God and to grow in our compassion for a hurting world.	*Good News About Injustice* chapters 2 and 5

 **REFLECT**

✳ Remembering the word *compassion* means "to suffer with," when have you suffered with others?

✳ Are there types of people you have trouble feeling compassion for? Explain.

—⟫⟫⟫ STUDY ⟪⟪⟪—

READ EXODUS 33:12–34:7.

¹²Moses said to the LORD, "You have been telling me, 'Lead these people,' but you have not let me know whom you will send with me. You have said, 'I know you by name and you have found favor with me.' ¹³If you are pleased with me, teach me your ways so I may know you and continue to find favor with you. Remember that this nation is your people."

¹⁴The LORD replied, "My Presence will go with you, and I will give you rest."

¹⁵Then Moses said to him, "If your Presence does not go with us, do not send us up from here. ¹⁶How will anyone know that you are pleased with me and with your people unless you go with us? What else will distinguish me and your people from all the other people on the face of the earth?"

¹⁷And the LORD said to Moses, "I will do the very thing you have asked, because I am pleased with you and I know you by name."

¹⁸Then Moses said, "Now show me your glory."

¹⁹And the LORD said, "I will cause all my goodness to pass in front of you, and I will proclaim my name, the LORD, in your presence. I will have mercy on whom I will have mercy, and I will have compassion on whom I will have compassion. ²⁰But," he said, "you cannot see my face, for no one may see me and live."

²¹Then the LORD said, "There is a place near me where you may stand on a rock. ²²When my glory passes by, I will put you in a cleft in the rock and cover you with my hand

until I have passed by. ²³Then I will remove my hand and you will see my back; but my face must not be seen."

CHAPTER 34

¹The Lord said to Moses, "Chisel out two stone tablets like the first ones, and I will write on them the words that were on the first tablets, which you broke. ²Be ready in the morning, and then come up on Mount Sinai. Present yourself to me there on top of the mountain. ³No one is to come with you or be seen anywhere on the mountain; not even the flocks and herds may graze in front of the mountain."

⁴So Moses chiseled out two stone tablets like the first ones and went up Mount Sinai early in the morning, as the Lord had commanded him; and he carried the two stone tablets in his hands. ⁵Then the Lord came down in the cloud and stood there with him and proclaimed his name, the Lord. ⁶And he passed in front of Moses, proclaiming, "The Lord, the Lord, the compassionate and gracious God, slow to anger, abounding in love and faithfulness, ⁷maintaining love to thousands, and forgiving wickedness, rebellion and sin. Yet he does not leave the guilty unpunished; he punishes the children and their children for the sin of the parents to the third and fourth generation."

1. By God's power, Moses and the people of Israel escaped slavery and Egypt. But they soon fell into idolatry, making a golden calf to worship. In his anger over the golden calf, Moses broke the tablets of the law God gave him. God then said he would not go with them into the Promised Land (Exodus 32:1–33:11). Now Moses is pleading with God to

continue with them on their journey. Moses makes three requests to God. What are the first two (33:12-13, 15-16)?

2. Why would these be important for Moses as well as for the people?

3. In 33:18 Moses follows up with an unusual request: "Now show me your glory." Why is this important in the context of what Moses has been asking?

> Glory is an image of divine transcendence that makes itself visible to people. It combines awe and terror, and it simultaneously invites approach and calls for distance. When Moses encounters the glory of God on Mt. Sinai, the visible manifestation is a cloud covering the mountain and brilliance "like a devouring fire" (Exodus 24:16-17 ESV). When Moses requests to see God's glory, it is so intense God has to shield him from the full effect (Exodus 33:18-23).[1]

4. How does God respond to the request in 33:19-23?

A cloud is a common image used throughout the Bible to indicate God's presence (Deuteronomy 33:26; 2 Samuel 22:10; Psalm 18:9; 68:4). The pillar of cloud led the people of Israel through the desert after they left Egypt (Exodus 13:22; 14:19, 24). A cloud also covered Mt. Sinai when the people of Israel gathered there and Moses went up to receive the Ten Commandments (Exodus 19:9, 16; 20:21; 24:15-18), and a cloud appeared at the tabernacle (Exodus 33:9-10; 40:34-38; Numbers 16:42). Exodus 16:10 equates the cloud with the Lord's presence. In 1 Kings 8:10, Isaiah 6:4, and Ezekiel 10:4, the temple is said to be filled with a cloud.[2]

5. What is revealed as God's glory in Exodus 34:5-7?

6. Compare this to what God says just a few verses earlier in 33:19-20. What is repeated, and why is this important?

7. While God's compassion is primary in this passage, it does not eliminate punishing the guilty (34:7). Why is it important that both of these aspects of God's character are included?

What is meant by "he punishes the children and their children for the sin of the parents to the third and fourth generation" (Exodus 34:7)? We who live in a world full of legacies of hate between colors, ethnic groups, and cultures can see only too clearly how sin in one generation affects those who follow even many generations later. So at least Moses must have understood the meaning: for he at once pleads both for pardon and for God's continued presence with his people (Exodus 34:8-9).[3]

RESPOND

✳ How does it give you hope to know that compassion is central to the essence of who our God is?

✳ Why is it important for us to pray that God be with us on our journey of faith as we seek to show compassion, graciousness, love, faithfulness, and forgiveness to a wicked and broken world?

PRAY

Compassionate and gracious God, we praise you that you are slow to anger, you abound in love and faithfulness, and you forgive wickedness and sin. We know all too well our sins of commission and of omission when it comes to those who suffer and who are oppressed. Thank you for the compassionate forgiveness you offer us and for the

compassionate care you offer them. May we become more like you in
those ways each day, for the glory of your name. Amen.

NEXT STEPS

✳ God's self-description found in Exodus 33:19 and 34:5-7 are
cornerstone passages recounting who God is. We find them
referred to again and again throughout the Bible. Here are
just a few passages to explore in context to gain a richer
understanding of this theme: Numbers 14:18; Nehemiah
9:17; Psalm 86:15; Psalm 103:8; Joel 2:13; Jonah 4:2; Micah
7:19; Nahum 1:3; Romans 9:15; James 5:11.

✳ Pray for front-line global workers who seek to bring freedom
to those who are enslaved in human trafficking, care to those
who are wrongfully imprisoned, and relief to those who
have been forcibly displaced from their homes by war. Pray
for all such workers in government and nongovernmental
agencies around the world who need emotional, physical,
and spiritual strength for these demanding tasks. Pray gov-
ernments, businesses, and individuals will give generously to
support these efforts financially.

---

[1]See "Glory," *Dictionary of Biblical Imagery*, ed. Leland Ryken, James C. Wilhoit, and
Tremper Longman III (Downers Grove, IL: IVP Academic, 1998), 330.

[2]Andrew T. Le Peau, *Mark Through Old Testament Eyes: A Background and Application Commentary* (Grand Rapids, MI: Kregel Academic, 2017), 160.

[3]See R. Alan Cole, *Exodus*, Tyndale Old Testament Commentaries (Downers Grove, IL:
IVP Academic, 1981), 238. Regarding a parallel use of this phrase in Deut 5:19, see also
J. G. McConville, *Deuteronomy*, Apollos Old Testament Commentary (Downers Grove,
IL: IVP Academic, 2002), 127.

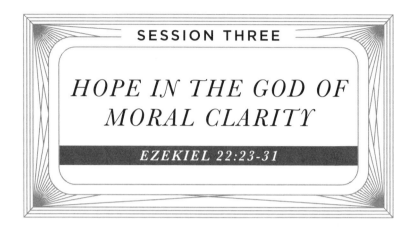

HOPE IN THE GOD OF MORAL CLARITY

EZEKIEL 22:23-31

THE BIBLE TELLS US THE God of justice has compassion for the victims of injustice, and we find hope in this truth. The Bible also tells us how God regards the perpetrators of injustice, and in this there is hope as well. We do not have a God who cannot distinguish between justice and injustice. Rather, Scripture makes wonderfully and dreadfully clear that God judges and condemns those who perpetrate injustice. Quite simply, our holy God has a burning wrath for those who use their power and authority to take from those who are weak.

God's wrath is out of fashion. It's not something we hear about, talk about, or even think about. Like animal sacrifices, God's intense and severe anger toward sin strikes us as rather primitive—something God has gotten over.

If we truly want to know God, we must endeavor to understand the holy God who has been made known in Scripture, the God who cannot accommodate the sin of injustice, who can't get used to it, who continually suffers with those who are brutalized in body and spirit by the arrogance of humans.

In fact, the knowledge of God's great anger toward and condemnation of injustice is what gives us hope to seek justice in this world. As we encounter the depravity of what people can do to each other, we have no words, no meaning, no life, no hope if there is not a God of history and time who is absolutely outraged, absolutely furious, absolutely burning with anger toward those who took it into their own hands to commit such acts.

In honest humility we must also understand that, as long as we are members of the human race, we are also capable of hatred and violence toward our neighbor, and we must also tremble as sinners before a holy God.

SESSION GOAL	READING
To find hope in a God who opposes and judges those who commit injustice.	*Good News About Injustice* chapters 3 and 6

 **REFLECT**

✳ Why are people sometimes embarrassed or troubled by the notion that God is full of anger and judgment?

✳ What acts of violence or injustice have you been angry and upset about?

 **STUDY**

READ EZEKIEL 22:23-31.

²³Again the word of the LORD came to me: ²⁴"Son of man, say to the land, 'You are a land that has not been cleansed

or rained on in the day of wrath.' [25]There is a conspiracy of her princes within her like a roaring lion tearing its prey; they devour people, take treasures and precious things and make many widows within her. [26]Her priests do violence to my law and profane my holy things; they do not distinguish between the holy and the common; they teach that there is no difference between the unclean and the clean; and they shut their eyes to the keeping of my Sabbaths, so that I am profaned among them. [27]Her officials within her are like wolves tearing their prey; they shed blood and kill people to make unjust gain. [28]Her prophets whitewash these deeds for them by false visions and lying divinations. They say, 'This is what the Sovereign LORD says'—when the LORD has not spoken. [29]The people of the land practice extortion and commit robbery; they oppress the poor and needy and mistreat the foreigner, denying them justice.

[30]"I looked for someone among them who would build up the wall and stand before me in the gap on behalf of the land so I would not have to destroy it, but I found no one. [31]So I will pour out my wrath on them and consume them with my fiery anger, bringing down on their own heads all they have done, declares the Sovereign LORD."

1. Ezekiel was called to be a prophet while in exile in Babylon following the defeat of Judah, around 600 BC. Much of his message was one of judgment against Judah for her many sins. In this passage, what different groups does Ezekiel condemn?

Rain, mentioned in verse 24, is considered
a special blessing in a land noted for drought.
In the Old Testament it is a sign of God's favor
(Deuteronomy 11:11; Psalm 147:8; Isaiah 55:10) and
its absence a sign of judgment on sin and rebellion
(Deuteronomy 28:22; Jeremiah 14:1-9; Joel 1:10-18).

2. What different sins has each group committed?

3. How do some of the religious leaders support these evil deeds (vv. 26 and 28)?

4. In what ways do we see religious leaders today sometimes attempting to whitewash sins committed by those in power?

5. Why are public and religious leaders especially accountable for what they do?

We often think of denying justice as a failure to punish wrongdoers, which it is. But verse 29 adds another dimension. Victims are said to be denied justice when they are extorted, oppressed, and mistreated.

6. Who today are the "poor and needy and . . . the foreigner" among us?

While you can define "poor and needy" in terms of material lack or lack of access to goods and services, it's important to remember victims of injustice are suffering because of intentional abuse and oppression by other people. This is a different problem than suffering because they don't have access to the gospel or don't have food or doctors or shelter, and it must be solved a different way. If we can address the problem of violence in communities, all other efforts of compassion and mercy will have an even greater chance at success.

7. What are examples of places where you see an abuse of power?

8. What do you think is God's plan for caring for those who are suffering today?

═══◣ **RESPOND** ◢═══

✳ What are the factors that make moral clarity difficult to achieve in our day?

✳ Is this a new problem?

✳ As you consider injustices done to the poor, needy, and foreigners, how do you gain hope by knowing God condemns such actions?

═══◣ **PRAY** ◢═══

O God of justice, who loves what is right and good, who hates violence, greed, and oppression, we thank you for standing with all victims of injustice and judging those who break your commands. Yet, like Isaiah, we know we are people of unclean lips who live among those of unclean lips. Thus your anger may rightly fall on us. We ask you to show mercy to those who repent and grant the grace for us to change our ways for the sake of your glory. Amen.

═══◣ **NEXT STEPS** ◢═══

✳ Frederick Buechner said, "The place God calls you to is the place where your deep gladness and the world's deep hunger meet." What are places of deep gladness for you?

✳ Now name places of deep hunger you see around you or in the world.

✳ How might these two places meet in your life?

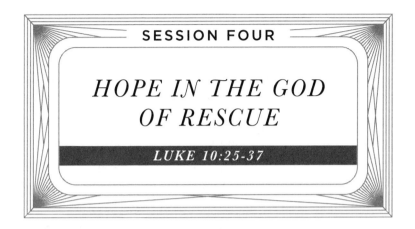

HOPE IN THE GOD OF RESCUE

LUKE 10:25-37

ACCORDING TO SCRIPTURE, God's justice, compassion, and righteousness manifest in an active, real-world response. This is not a God who offers sympathy, best wishes, or cruel character-building exercises. This is a God who wants evildoers brought to account and vulnerable people protected—here and now!

> But you, God, see the trouble of the afflicted;
>   you consider their grief and take it in hand.
> The victims commit themselves to you;
>   you are the helper of the fatherless. (Psalm 10:14)

Knowing the pain is real, God doesn't spiritualize the suffering of injustice. God knows the whip is real, the fist hurts, torture kills, and injustice can so brutalize our spirit as to make us feel forsaken by the heavenly Father.

God knows that, ultimately, lost souls need a Savior and "our struggle is not against flesh and blood, but against the rulers, against the authorities, against the powers of this dark world and against the spiritual forces of evil in the heavenly realms" (Ephesians 6:12). But God also clearly knows that the powers of darkness and forces of evil can manifest themselves on this earth as real hunger, real nakedness, real imprisonment, real beatings, and real injustice.

While never neglecting or subordinating spiritual needs, Jesus calls his followers to respond to hunger with food, to nakedness with clothes, to imprisonment with visitation, to beatings with bandages, and to injustice with justice (Matthew 15:32-38; 25:35-36; Luke 10:34; 11:42). As the apostle James wrote, "Suppose a brother or a sister is without clothes and daily food. If one of you says to them, 'Go in peace; keep warm and well fed,' but does nothing about their physical needs, what good is it?" (James 2:15-16).

SESSION GOAL	READING
To see how God is a God of rescue for victims of injustice and for all of us.	*Good News About Injustice* chapters 7–9

 **REFLECT**

✳ In what ways do you see the God of rescue at work in the world today?

✳ How do you respond to the words of James quoted above (James 2:15-16)?

STUDY

READ LUKE 10:25-37.

²⁵On one occasion an expert in the law stood up to test Jesus. "Teacher," he asked, "what must I do to inherit eternal life?"

²⁶"What is written in the Law?" he replied. "How do you read it?"

²⁷He answered, "'Love the Lord your God with all your heart and with all your soul and with all your strength and with all your mind'; and, 'Love your neighbor as yourself.'"

²⁸"You have answered correctly," Jesus replied. "Do this and you will live."

²⁹But he wanted to justify himself, so he asked Jesus, "And who is my neighbor?"

³⁰In reply Jesus said: "A man was going down from Jerusalem to Jericho, when he was attacked by robbers. They stripped him of his clothes, beat him and went away, leaving him half dead. ³¹A priest happened to be going down the same road, and when he saw the man, he passed by on the other side. ³²So too, a Levite, when he came to the place and saw him, passed by on the other side. ³³But a Samaritan, as he traveled, came where the man was; and when he saw him, he took pity on him. ³⁴He went to him and bandaged his wounds, pouring on oil and wine. Then he put the man on his own donkey, brought him to an inn and took care of him. ³⁵The next day he took out two denarii and gave them to the innkeeper. 'Look after him,' he said, 'and when I return, I will reimburse you for any extra expense you may have.'

³⁶"Which of these three do you think was a neighbor to the man who fell into the hands of robbers?"

³⁷The expert in the law replied, "The one who had mercy on him."

Jesus told him, "Go and do likewise."

1. This passage has two rounds of questioning on slightly different issues. What is the main topic in Luke 10:25-28, and what is it in 10:29-37?

2. The lawyer intended to test Jesus (v. 25). How does Jesus turn this exchange into a test for the lawyer?

> The seventeen-mile descending desert road from Jerusalem to Jericho had a reputation for being dangerous. Thieves found the terrain ideal for attacking travelers. Leaving an injured person on the road could also have been bait for an ambush when someone stopped to help.

3. How would Jesus' listeners expect the priest and the Levite to act upon seeing the injured man?

4. Consider two groups: the robbers on the one hand, and the priest and Levite on the other. How does each person use their power? How are they different from one another, and how are they similar?

The US civil rights leader Martin Luther King Jr. would often refer to the Jericho Road in his sermons. He would say he didn't just want to be the Good Samaritan—he was tired of seeing people battered, bruised, and bloody along the dangerous Jericho Roads of life. Instead he wanted to fix the road, pave it, and add streetlights to allow everyone safe passage. (See Dr. King's final speech, "I've Been to the Mountaintop," and other sermons.)

5. Why is the Samaritan an unexpected hero in this parable?

Samaritans claimed to be a remnant of the Northern Kingdom of Israel that stayed in the land after the rest of the nation was taken into exile by Assyria and Babylon. Because of historical tensions and of differences regarding the true place of worship, Jews and Samaritans had been at odds for hundreds of years.

6. Jesus changed the topic of the first question (v. 25) from one of knowing the law to one of doing the law. Jesus makes a similar move in the second round. He uses the parable to transform the lawyer's second question from "Who is my neighbor?" into "Who acted like a good neighbor?" How would you answer that second question?

7. How do I use my power in response to the vulnerability I see around me?

 **RESPOND**

✳ How does it give you hope to think about the Samaritan as a picture of Christ for us?

✳ How do you respond to knowing that even in the work of fighting injustice, we do not have to be perfect or to do it on our own, but Christ is there to carry us on our way?

PRAY

O God of Rescue, we thank you that you have compassion and show mercy to all the weak. We thank you that, though we are helpless and half dead, you have come to heal our wounds, bring us to safety, and pay for all our needs. We ask you now to come and help us care for those who are abused, hurting, and lonely, who have little physical, emotional, and spiritual support from the world. We ask for the sake of your glory and name. Amen.

NEXT STEPS

"Do not be deceived: God cannot be mocked. A man reaps what he sows. Whoever sows to please their flesh, from the flesh will reap destruction; whoever sows to please the Spirit, from the Spirit will reap eternal life. Let us not become weary in doing good, for at the proper time we will reap a harvest if we do not give up" (Galatians 6:7-9). It is easy to be overwhelmed by the needs around us, in our country and in the world. What does it mean, as we face injustice, that we can be certain God will not be mocked? How can we pursue justice without "growing weary"? Brainstorm a few ideas that could restore, refresh, and renew you and others in following God's lead. Then pick one you can put into practice this week.

Now write a short prayer asking God to sustain you and others as you seek to confront injustice at home and abroad. Thank God for the renewal, healing, and refreshment he brings.

WORSHIPING THE GOD OF JUSTICE

MICAH 6:1-8

HISTORIANS HAVE LONG RECOGNIZED that the great achievements in humanitarian reform and social justice during the nineteenth century—the abolition of slavery, prison reform, the establishment of hospitals and schools for the poor, women's rights, opposition to forced prostitution, the fight against child labor and for civil rights—were largely built on the faithful zeal of Christians.

For 2,000 years, Christians have been trying to make it believable that God is good. If some people are suffering because they don't have access to the gospel, we go and share the story of God's love with them. If others are suffering because they don't have food, we help them with food. If they're suffering without doctors or medicine, we share ours. When we do that, they actually see us, the body of Christ, show up and it becomes believable to them that God is good!

But for the last 150 years, until only recently, Christians have largely forgotten the work of justice as a key part of their witness in the world. Christ now calls us to recover the ministry of justice that once was ours. In the words of Katharine Bushnell, an anti-trafficking activist, medical doctor, Christian writer,

Bible scholar, and forerunner of feminist theology in the late eighteenth century and early nineteenth century,

> There is absolutely nothing which destroys morality out of the human heart so effectually and quickly as injustice, and there is nothing which so quickly lights the Divine flame of penitence and aspiration for holiness, in the heart of the fallen, as the hope of justice. Justice is the kindest thing in the world; injustice is the cruelest and the most depressing.[1]

Social justice is fully consistent with a holistic view of the church and its mission. Justice is integral to the heart of God's plan for the world—and it turns out we are his plan for seeking justice. Scripture is clear we are God's plan for making it believable that he is good to those who are suffering (Matthew 5:14-16). And God doesn't have another plan. As we peer down the halls of Christian history, we give thanks for those great champions of justice who give us hope. God equips people "to act justly and to love mercy and to walk humbly" (Micah 6:8) and desires for us to remember and sustain this ancient work throughout time.

SESSION GOAL	READING
To grow in the kind of worship God desires.	*Good News About Injustice* chapters 10–13

REFLECT

✳ What have been some of your most memorable experiences of worship?

✳ How would you define worship of God?

STUDY

READ MICAH 6:1-8.

¹Listen to what the Lord says:
"Stand up, plead my case before the mountains;
   let the hills hear what you have to say.
²"Hear, you mountains, the Lord's accusation;
   listen, you everlasting foundations of the earth.
For the Lord has a case against his people;
   he is lodging a charge against Israel.
³"My people, what have I done to you?
   How have I burdened you? Answer me.
⁴I brought you up out of Egypt
   and redeemed you from the land of slavery.
I sent Moses to lead you,
   also Aaron and Miriam.
⁵My people, remember
   what Balak king of Moab plotted
   and what Balaam son of Beor answered.
Remember your journey from Shittim to Gilgal,
   that you may know the righteous acts of the Lord."
⁶With what shall I come before the Lord
   and bow down before the exalted God?
Shall I come before him with burnt offerings,
   with calves a year old?
⁷Will the Lord be pleased with thousands of rams,
   with ten thousand rivers of olive oil?

Shall I offer my firstborn for my transgression,
>   the fruit of my body for the sin of my soul?
⁸He has shown you, O mortal, what is good.
>   And what does the LORD require of you?
To act justly and to love mercy
>   and to walk humbly with your God.

Micah was a prophet of the southern kingdom of Judah, during the reigns of Jotham, Ahaz, and Hezekiah (about 740 to 690 BC). He prophesied judgment on Samaria and Judah (1:1-16) because of their many sins. Rulers seized homes, land, and property from widows, orphans, travelers, and other weak members of society (2:2, 8-9; 3:1-3), and judges took bribes (3:11). But Micah also promised rescue from their enemies and that God's kingdom would come with mercy and justice (4:1-5:15).

1. In Micah 6, God is on trial. Instead of doing them wrong, what does the Lord say in his defense? What has God done for the people of Israel (6:3-5)?

Micah mentions Balak, Baalam, Shittim, and Gilgal. As the people of Israel prepared to enter the Promised Land, Moab and Midian united against them. Their king, Balak, hired the prophet Baalam to curse Israel. But an angel appeared to Baalam and commanded him to bless Israel instead (Numbers 22-24). The people traveled from Shittim, crossing the Jordan, to Gilgal, the first place they stayed in the Promised Land (Joshua 4:19).

2. The Lord says all these acts revealed his righteousness (6:5). How did they do that?

3. In 6:6-7, what does Micah say are possible responses to these acts of God?

4. What is the prophet trying to communicate by the extreme size of the responses he contemplates, far beyond what the Old Testament law calls for?

> Sacrifices for sin were to be part of the regular rituals of Israel (Leviticus 4:1-35; 9:3-4). But another prominent theme in the Old Testament is that God prefers obedience more than sacrifices (1 Samuel 15:22; Psalm 40:6-8; Proverbs 21:3; Hosea 6:6), a theme Jesus reiterates (Matthew 9:13; 12:7; Mark 12:33).

5. How does Micah instead suggest the people respond to God's goodness and their sin?

6. What connection do you see between Christians showing the love of God to people in desperate need and how that might help someone come to know the goodness of God?

7. What do these passages reveal about God's view of justice and mercy as an expression of true worship?

8. Many churches have strong disagreements about what particular forms worship should take. How, in light of this passage, might this show our priorities are misaligned?

9. Micah says three things are required: "To act justly and to love mercy and to walk humbly with your God" (6:8). How is "walking humbly with your God" connected to the other two?

RESPOND

✳ Why do you think it is that in many churches more energy is expended on doing worship "just the right way" in comparison to obeying God's call to mercy and justice?

✳ When have you experienced a connection between worship and doing justice? Explain.

PRAY

Father in heaven, we have not worshiped you as we ought. We have sung songs and prayed prayers, but we have too often failed to care for those who have fallen victim to the trials of life. May you forgive us, renew our hearts, and strengthen us to do your will of supporting widows and orphans, helping the poor, opposing corruption and greed, feeding the hungry, welcoming the stranger, lifting the burdens of the oppressed, and caring for the weak. May we take joy in giving you true worship in these ways and by your power. Amen.

NEXT STEPS

✳ How is your church already tangibly helping people who are suffering from violent injustice or abuse?

✳ What ways might you be able to join in or initiate such efforts?

✳ How could you or your church better combine worship times and showing mercy?

✳ Investigate the many options and resources International Justice Mission has for individuals, churches, students, businesses, and volunteers at ijm.org.

---

[1]Katharine C. Bushnell, *God's Word to Women: One Hundred Bible Studies on Woman's Place in the Church and Home* (1921; reprint, Minneapolis, MN: Christians for Biblical Equality, 2003), 302.

LEADING A SMALL GROUP

LEADING A BIBLE DISCUSSION can be an enjoyable and re-
warding experience. But it can also be intimidating—especially
if you've never done it before. If this is how you feel, you're in
good company.

Remember when God asked Moses to lead the Israelites out
of Egypt? Moses replied, "Please send someone else" (Exodus
4:13)! But God gave Moses the help (human and divine) he
needed to be a strong leader.

Leading a Bible discussion is not difficult if you follow certain
guidelines. You don't need to be an expert on the Bible or a
trained teacher. The suggestions listed below can help you to
effectively fulfill your role as leader—and enjoy doing it.

PREPARING FOR THE STUDY

1. As you study the passage before the group meeting, ask God
   to help you understand it and apply it in your own life. Unless
   this happens, you will not be prepared to lead others. Pray too
   for the various members of the group. Ask God to open your
   hearts to the message of his Word and motivate you to action.

2. Read the introduction to the entire guide to get an overview of the subject at hand and the issues that will be explored.

3. Be ready to respond to the "Reflect" questions with a personal story or example. The group will be only as vulnerable and open as its leader.

4. Read the chapters of the companion book that are recommended at the beginning of the session.

5. Read and reread the assigned Bible passage to familiarize yourself with it. You may want to look up the passage in a Bible so that you can see its context.

6. This study guide is based on the New International Version of the Bible. It will help you and the group if you use this translation as the basis for your study and discussion.

7. Carefully work through each question in the study. Spend time in meditation and reflection as you consider how to respond.

8. Write your thoughts and responses in the space provided in the study guide. This will help you to express your understanding of the passage clearly.

9. It might help you to have a Bible dictionary handy. Use it to look up any unfamiliar words, names, or places.

10. Take the final (application) study questions and the "Respond" portion of each study seriously. Consider what this means for your life, what changes you may need to make in your lifestyle, or what actions you can take in your church or with people you know. Remember that the group will follow your lead in responding to the studies.

LEADING THE STUDY

1. Be sure everyone in your group has a study guide and a Bible. Encourage the group to prepare beforehand for each discussion by reading the introduction to the guide and by working through the questions for that session.

2. At the beginning of your first time together, explain that these studies are meant to be discussions, not lectures. Encourage the members of the group to participate. However, do not put pressure on those who may be hesitant to speak during the first few sessions.

3. Begin the study on time. Open with prayer, asking God to help the group understand and apply the passage.

4. Have a group member read aloud the introductory paragraphs at the beginning of the discussion. This will remind the group of the topic of the study.

5. Discuss the "Reflect" questions before reading the Bible passage. These kinds of opening questions are important for several reasons. First, there is usually a stiffness that needs to be overcome before people will begin to talk openly. A good question will break the ice.

   Second, most people will have lots of different things going on in their minds (dinner, an exam, an important meeting coming up, how to get the car fixed) that have nothing to do with the study. A creative question will get their attention and draw them into the discussion.

   Third, opening questions can reveal where our thoughts or feelings need to be transformed by Scripture. That is why it is important not to read the passage before the "Reflect" questions are asked. The passage will tend to color the honest reactions people would otherwise give, because they feel they are supposed to think the way the Bible does.

6. Have a group member read aloud the Scripture passage.

7. As you ask the questions, keep in mind that they are designed to be used just as they are written. You may simply read them aloud. Or you may prefer to express them in your own words.

   There may be times when it is appropriate to deviate from the study guide. For example, a question may already have been answered. If so, move on to the next question. Or someone may raise an important question not covered in the guide. Take time to discuss it, but try to keep the group from going off on tangents.

8. Avoid offering the first answer to a study question. Repeat or rephrase questions if necessary until they are clearly understood. An eager group quickly becomes passive and silent if members think the leader will give all the *right* answers.

9. Don't be afraid of silence. People may need time to think about the question before formulating their answers.

10. Don't be content with just one answer. Ask, "What do the rest of you think?" or, "Anything else?" until several people have given answers to a question. You might point out one of the study sidebars to help spur discussion; for example, "Does the quotation on page seventeen provide any insight as you think about this question?"

11. Acknowledge all contributions. Be affirming whenever possible. Never reject an answer. If it is clearly off-base, ask, "Which verse led you to that conclusion?" or, "What do the rest of you think?"

12. Don't expect every answer to be addressed to you, even though this will probably happen at first. As group members become more at ease, they will begin to truly interact with each other. This is one sign of healthy discussion.

13. Don't be afraid of controversy. It can be stimulating! If you don't resolve an issue completely, don't be frustrated. Move on and keep it in mind for later. A subsequent study may solve the problem.

14. Try to periodically summarize what the group has said about the passage. This helps to draw together the various ideas mentioned and gives continuity to the study. But don't preach.

15. When you come to the application questions at the end of each "Study" section, be willing to keep the discussion going by describing how you have been affected by the study. It's important that we each apply the message of the passage to ourselves in a specific way.

    Depending on the makeup of your group and the length of time you've been together, you may or may not want to discuss the "Respond" section. If not, allow the group to read it and reflect on it silently. Encourage members to make specific commitments and to write them in their study guide. Ask them the following week how they did with their commitments.

16. Conclude your time together with conversational prayer. Ask for God's help in following through on the commitments you've made.

17. End the group discussion on time.

Many more suggestions and helps are found in The Big Book on Small Groups *by Jeffrey Arnold.*

SUGGESTED RESOURCES BY INTERNATIONAL JUSTICE MISSION

George, Abraham, and Nikki A. Toyama-Szeto.
God of Justice: The IJM Institute Global Church Curriculum.
Downers Grove, IL: InterVarsity Press, 2015.

Haugen, Gary A. *Good News About Injustice:
A Witness of Courage in a Hurting World.*
Downers Grove, IL: InterVarsity Press, 1999, 2009.

Haugen, Gary A. *Just Courage: God's Great Expedition for the
Restless Christian.* Downers Grove, IL: InterVarsity Press, 2008.

Haugen, Gary A., and Victor Boutros. *The Locust Effect:
Why the End of Poverty Requires the End of Violence.*
New York: Oxford University Press, 2015.

Haugen, Gary A., with Gregg Hunter. *Terrify No More: Young
Girls Held Captive and the Daring Undercover Operation to Win
Their Freedom.* Nashville, TN: W Publishing Group, 2005.

Hoang, Bethany Hanke. *Deepening the Soul for Justice.*
Downers Grove, IL: InterVarsity Press, 2012.

Hoang, Bethany Hanke, and Kristen Deede Johnson. *The Justice Calling: Where Passion Meets Perseverance.* Grand Rapids, MI: Brazos Press, 2017.

Martin, Jim. *The Just Church: Becoming a Risk-Taking, Justice-Seeking, Disciple-Making Congregation.* Carol Stream, IL: Tyndale Momentum, 2012.

For additional resources on justice and Christian life, see appendix 4 of *Good News About Injustice*.

THE IVP SIGNATURE COLLECTION

Since 1947 InterVarsity Press has been publishing thoughtful Christian books that serve the university, the church, and the world. In celebration of our seventy-fifth anniversary, IVP is releasing special editions of select iconic and bestselling books from throughout our history.

RELEASED IN 2019

Basic Christianity (1958)
JOHN STOTT

How to Give Away Your Faith (1966)
PAUL E. LITTLE

RELEASED IN 2020

The God Who Is There (1968)
FRANCIS A. SCHAEFFER

This Morning with God (1968)
EDITED BY CAROL ADENEY AND BILL WEIMER

The Fight (1976)
JOHN WHITE

Free at Last? (1983)
CARL F. ELLIS JR.

The Dust of Death (1973)
OS GUINNESS

The Singer (1975)
CALVIN MILLER

RELEASED IN 2021

Knowing God (1973)
J. I. PACKER

Out of the Saltshaker and Into the World (1979) REBECCA MANLEY PIPPERT

A Long Obedience in the Same Direction (1980) EUGENE H. PETERSON

More Than Equals (1993)
SPENCER PERKINS AND CHRIS RICE

Between Heaven and Hell (1982)
PETER KREEFT

Good News About Injustice (1999)
GARY A. HAUGEN

The Challenge of Jesus (1999)
N. T. WRIGHT

Hearing God (1999)
DALLAS WILLARD

RELEASING IN 2022

The Heart of Racial Justice (2004)
BRENDA SALTER McNEIL AND RICK RICHARDSON

Sacred Rhythms (2006)
RUTH HALEY BARTON

Habits of the Mind (2000)
JAMES W. SIRE

True Story (2008)
JAMES CHOUNG

Scribbling in the Sand (2002)
MICHAEL CARD

The Next Worship (2015)
SANDRA MARIA VAN OPSTAL

Delighting in the Trinity (2012)
MICHAEL REEVES

Strong and Weak (2016)
ANDY CROUCH

Liturgy of the Ordinary (2016)
TISH HARRISON WARREN

IVP SIGNATURE BIBLE STUDIES

As companions to the IVP Signature Collection, IVP Signature Bible Studies feature the inductive study method, equipping individuals and groups to explore the biblical truths embedded in these books.

Basic Christianity Bible Study
JOHN STOTT

How to Give Away Your Faith Bible Study
PAUL E. LITTLE

The Singer Bible Study, CALVIN MILLER

Knowing God Bible Study, J. I. PACKER

A Long Obedience in the Same Direction Bible Study, EUGENE H. PETERSON

Good News About Injustice Bible Study
GARY A. HAUGEN

Hearing God Bible Study
DALLAS WILLARD

The Heart of Racial Justice Bible Study
BRENDA SALTER McNEIL AND
RICK RICHARDSON

True Story Bible Study, JAMES CHOUNG

The Next Worship Bible Study
SANDRA MARIA VAN OPSTAL

Strong and Weak Bible Study
ANDY CROUCH